GERMS
DISEASE-CAUSING ORGANISMS™

PARASITES

MARGAUX BAUM and JENNIFER VIEGAS

rosen publishing's
rosen central®

Published in 2017 by The Rosen Publishing Group, Inc.
29 East 21st Street, New York, NY 10010

Library of Congress Cataloging-in-Publication Data
Names: Baum, Margaux, author. | Viegas, Jennifer, author.
Title: Parasites / Margaux Baum and Jennifer Viegas.
Description: First edition. | New York : Rosen Central, 2017. | Series:
 Germs: disease causing organisms | Audience: Grades 5-8. | Includes
 bibliographical references and index.
Identifiers: LCCN 2016002007| ISBN 9781477788493 (library bound) | ISBN
 9781477788479 (pbk.) | ISBN 9781477788486 (6-pack)
Subjects: LCSH: Parasites--Juvenile literature.
Classification: LCC QL757 .V52 2017 | DDC 591.6/5--dc23
LC record available at http://lccn.loc.gov/2016002007

Manufactured in China

CONTENTS

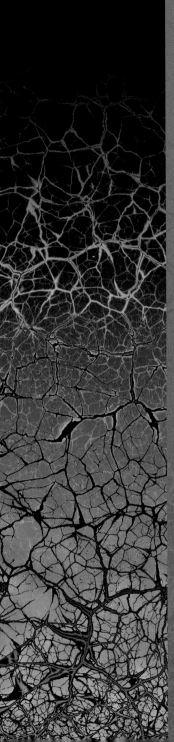

INTRODUCTION

All around us, largely unseen, a kind of creature exists that is both repulsive and fascinating to laypeople and scientists alike: parasites.

The ancient Greeks and Romans first coined the term parasite—in Greek, *parásitos*; in Latin, *parasītus*—and for both civilizations, the word had a host of negative meanings: one who eats at another's table and also an uninvited dinner guest. For modern English speakers, the word can mean any person who takes and does not give and is often used in disgust.

Many people believe they know what parasites are, but may be surprised by what living things are classified as such. Some common pests humans try to avoid, and even kill in many circumstances, are insects that we may unknowingly classify as parasites, such as mosquitoes, horseflies, and other biting and harmful insects, even though they are not.

At the same time, some diseases and infections that we might casually dismiss as viral or bacterial in nature may actually have parasites as their root cause, such as the tiny organisms that enter our digestive systems. Even one very common sexually transmitted disease (STD), trichomoniasis, is actually caused by the parasitic organism Trichomonas vaginalis.

Parisitism may seem like an unusual lifestyle for organisms, but in reality it is one of the most common on Earth. While parasites are an annoyance and inconvenience for many sufferers in the developed West, they are a life and death matter for those in less developed countries. A parasitic microorganism causes malaria, for example. This is a disease that, according to the World Health Organization (WHO), accounted for at least 214 million new cases in 2015, with 438,000 deaths.

Parasitic relationships exist across many different species and are believed to be behind recent troubling phenomena. For example, scientists theorize that massive die-offs of honey-bees in Europe and North America may be at least partially due to parasitic infections from a type of mite.

Wherever they exist, parasites range from relatively harmless and common, to catastrophically destructive, as in the case of malaria. In this book, we will define and identify what makes an organism parasitic and explore the unique relationships between parasites and their hosts. The types of parasites will be discussed, including the microorganisms known as protozoa, tiny insects, and larger parasites such as lice and intestinal worms. Learning about these living beings will hopefully provide readers an understanding of their unique adaptations and their place in the huge, complex, and interconnected web of life around us.

CHAPTER 1

DEFINING AND IDENTIFYING PARASITES

Most living things depend on other organisms for survival. Human beings, as with other creatures, depend on other organisms as food sources, whether plant life or animal flesh. Humans are omnivores, which means they can eat both types of food, and in their role as consumers of meat, they are predators.

Parasites have a slightly different mode of survival. They not only feed on other organisms, but they also live in or on their bodies.

The animal providing food and shelter for a parasite is called a host. Usually the host is much bigger than the parasite. A larger creature can provide great benefits for a parasite, such as an enormous food supply, tissues that give the parasite protection and warmth, and the mobility to get around and find more hosts.

It is in the best interest of a parasite to keep its host alive since the host's well-being directly affects the parasite. If the host dies, the parasite might die, too, or at least have to find another host. But parasites are usually fairly simple organisms that act without self-awareness. If they make a host fatally ill, they must move on or die. Many parasites have a complex life cycle that involves moving through several different environments and hosts.

Sometimes the connection between a host and a parasite is an example of symbiosis. The word "symbiosis" means "living together," and in scientific terms it refers to a close relationship between two distinct organisms that benefits both. A colony of ants finds shelter inside a tree. But they also protect the tree from leaf-eating insects. That is a symbiotic relationship. But in pure parasitism, the host gets nothing from the presence of the parasite.

There are many different kinds of parasites. Some can be viewed only through a microscope. Others can grow to be several feet long. All can be divided into three basic groups: protozoa, worms, and parasitic insects and arachnids.

If you experience stomach cramps, bloating, gas, burping, weakness, and loss of appetite, you may have giardiasis, caused by this flagellated protozoan, *Giardia lamblia*.

PROTOZOA

Microscopic, single-celled organisms are called protozoa. These tiny creatures are neither plant nor animal but are classified as somewhere in between. The word "protozoan" is derived from the Greek word for "first," *protos*, referring to the fact that these organisms are some of Earth's simplest life-forms and were probably among the first living creatures to evolve on the planet.

Not all protozoa are parasites. Many, particularly those that thrive in water, do just fine on their own as long as they are in the right environment. Amoebas, for example, derive their food and oxygen from the water in which they live. Some protozoa are green in color because, like plants, they have organelles containing chlorophyll, which produce food from sunlight. Still other protozoa do need a host in order to survive, making them parasites.

Protozoa can be divided into four categories: flagellates, sarcodines, apicomplexans, and ciliates. Flagellates possess hairlike appendages that enable them to move quickly and smoothly through water. Many are harmless, but some, like the group called the trypanosomes, can cause disease.

Sarcodines use pseudopods, or "false feet," to move. The pseudopod resembles a miniature toe. Some sarcodines can cause disease when ingested but many are harmless. One ocean group even grows a chalky skeleton that the creatures shed. Over time, the skeletons build up and create structures similar to the shells that other animals use for shelter.

Unlike flagellates and sarcodines, all apicomplexans are parasites. They move by gliding through their environment. A number of apicomplexans can be quite dangerous to humans. Malaria, for example, is caused by an apicomplexan parasite.

Ciliates are like flagellates in that they also possess hairy growths on the exterior of their cells to help them move. More developed in structure, however, ciliates are the most complex form of protozoan. They may have other complex anatomical features to help them survive, such as tubes that aid in feeding.

PARASITIC WORMS

Worms are animals that possess a soft, thin body without a backbone or limbs. You have likely seen worms in your backyard or at a park. That is because worms often live in soil or water. Many are very essential to their environments, serving as cleanup crews and adding beneficial nutrients to the soil. Parasitic worms, on the other hand, can pose a danger to plants, humans, and animals. In the best case, a parasitic worm feeds off of its host without the host even knowing that the worm is present. In the worst case, blood and nutrients can be lost, leading to health disorders.

Worms are divided into four primary groups: flatworms, ribbon worms, roundworms, and segmented worms. Flatworms indeed are flat but come in different shapes. Some are narrow, while others grow in an oval form. Flatworms and other worms that do not live as parasites are free to move about in the soil or water and have a variety of food sources. Parasitic flatworms, like flukes and tapeworms, rely on other creatures for their nourishment. They can pose serious health problems to humans and other animals.

Ribbon worms are like flatworms, only larger. In fact, some ribbon worms can grow to become several feet long. Many are parasitic, feeding on animals and even other worms.

Roundworms possess long, tubular bodies. This is the largest group of worms, with approximately twelve thousand species. Most free-living species inhabit the water and soil and are perfectly harmless. Parasitic roundworms, however, can hurt their hosts by causing disease.

The bodies of segmented worms are divided into sections that look like rings. Again, many are harmless to humans but some, like leeches, feed off the blood of their hosts.

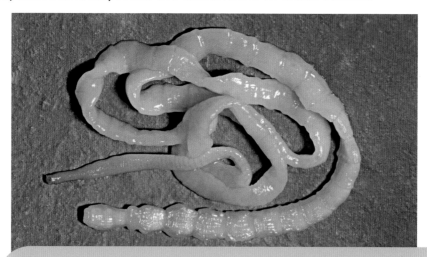

This tapeworm (*Dipylidium caninum*) exited from a cat's mouth after it was given medicine to treat the creature's infestation. This kind of tapeworm can also afflict dogs and even small children.

INSECTS AND ARACHNIDS: MULTILEGGED PARASITES

Insects are small, air-breathing animals that are invertebrates, meaning that they do not have backbones. They are usually characterized by their six legs and bodies divided into three parts. A unique feature is their exoskeleton, a hard shell covering their soft body parts. They may or may not have wings. Arachnids are a type of animal with eight jointed legs and segmented bodies. Spiders are one common arachnid, but the group also includes ticks and mites, which are parasitic.

Except for one species of mite that lays its eggs in human skin, insect parasites and arachnids live on the skin instead of inside the bodies of their hosts. Fleas and lice are common parasitic insects. Ticks are common parasitic arachnids. They have mouthparts that enable them to attach themselves to the skin, where they can draw out nutrients.

While mites, fleas, ticks, and lice tend to target one species as hosts, another group of insects prefers to take a small amount of blood from a number of different hosts. They are known as blood-sucking micropredators. Biting flies, such as tsetse flies, sand flies, and black flies, are micropredators, along with mosquitoes. Technically they are not parasites, but they can carry protozoan parasites in their bodies and spread disease.

PARASITES

This deer tick, engorged with blood, can potentially be a carrier of several different diseases that harm humans, including ehrlichiosis, babesiosis, Rocky Mountain spotted fever, and Lyme disease.

Many insects live free for part of their lives and are parasitic at other times. For example, fleas begin life as eggs. When hatched, the larvae are not parasites. When the fleas become adults, they become parasites.

FREELOADING FISH AND SHARKS

Sharks are one of nature's toughest predators, so why are they often seen accompanied by groups of tiny fish? Usually these fish are remoras, also known as shark suckers or sucker fish. These fish possess tiny suction cups on the tops of their heads. Remoras literally attach themselves to the undersides or bellies of sharks and hitch free rides. In addition, the remoras gain protection from predators and feed off of scraps that fly from the shark's mouth. In return, it is believed that remoras remove and consume parasites from the shark's body. For some time, scientists have debated whether the presence of remoras was an example of commensalism (a relationship in which one organism benefits from a host without affecting it), or mutualism (in which both organisms benefit from each other), with more evidence pointing to the latter interpretation.

MUTUALISM

One form of symbiosis is mutualism. In mutualism, both parties in a relationship derive mutual benefits from it. The case of blue-green algae and a fungus provides one of the more notable examples of mutualism. When these two organisms interact, they can combine into an entirely new, or composite, organism called lichen. Its characteristics differ greatly from those of its parent organisms. The fungus part absorbs and retains moisture, while the algae's chlorophyll works to manufacture the organism's food. The newly formed lichen thrives even in the most inhospitable environments.

CHAPTER 2

PROTOZOA AND INSECTS

There are many things that can make human beings sick. Some of the root causes of ill health are factors that threaten the human body's homeostasis, the stability of its internal conditions. Imbalance in our bodies can cause them to malfunction, and parasites are among the culprits that cause such imbalances, along with other diseases and extreme environmental factors. A flu virus will elevate a person's body temperature, at times even fatally, and this imbalance is a sign of the body fighting the viral infection.

Protozoa are different from viruses. Viruses are inert, meaning that they do not have the power to move on their own, an ability that protozoa possess. Parasitic protozoa that cause illness and disease in animals and humans are pathogenic. A pathogenic parasite benefits at the expense of its host.

Each year in the United States, thousands of people become ill as a result of ingesting parasitic protozoa. It is important to remember that protozoa are microscopic creatures, meaning that they can be viewed only under a microscope.

Water, food, and soil containing the parasites may not appear to have any outward signs of contamination. Humans usually suffer from protozoan disease after having ingested contaminated water and food. Both of these sources harbor different types of parasites.

PARASITES IN WATER

Waterborne disease is still fairly common in this country, with many states reporting illnesses each year. Two of the most common diseases caused by protozoa in water are giardiasis (pronounced gee-are-dye-uh-sis) and cryptosporidiosis (krip-toe-spo-rid-ee-oh-sis). Both get their names from the parasitic protozoa that cause the illnesses.

Giardiasis occurs when a person or animal becomes infected with a parasite called *Giardia lamblia*. This parasite can be found in soil, food, and water, and on moist, contaminated surfaces. Ingesting water containing the parasite is a common way in which giardiasis is spread. Frequently, water will contain sewage or feces that harbor the parasites. *Giardia lamblia* is especially hearty and can survive in a dormant state for extended periods of time. That is because the parasite is covered with a protective outer shell. It is impossible to detect in water unless viewed under a microscope.

Symptoms of giardiasis include diarrhea and other intestinal problems, stomach cramps, and sometimes nausea,

PARASITES

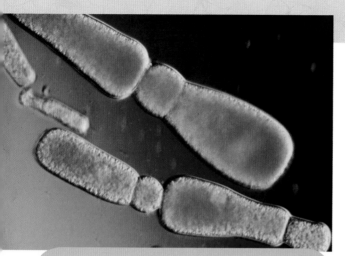

These two gregarines, each measuring about a half a millimeter long, get ready for syzygy, or reproduction. Gregarines inhabit the intestines of invertebrates.

dehydration, and weight loss. Symptoms usually last anywhere from two to six weeks but may last longer. Sometimes outbreaks occur after flooding, when sewage or waste runoff enters the water supply. A person can also become infected after swallowing contaminated water found in improperly treated swimming pools, hot tubs, Jacuzzis, fountains, or in natural settings such as lakes, rivers, springs, ponds, and streams. Giardiasis is usually treatable with prescription drugs.

A tiny parasite called *Cryptosporidium parvum* causes the diarrheal disease cryptosporidiosis, better known as crypto. Similar to the giardiasis parasite, the crypto parasite possesses a shell that enables it to survive outside of its host or in certain environments for long periods.

Crypto is spread like giardiasis and has similar symptoms. The main difference is that with crypto, the symptoms usually become apparent two to ten days after the victim is infected. The illness may then persist for a couple of weeks, during which time the sick person may go through cycles of feeling better and feeling worse before the illness finally goes away completely.

FOODBORNE PROTOZOA

Food, like water, can provide an environment in which parasites can live and wait for a host, such as an unsuspecting hungry human. Two parasitic diseases commonly spread through contaminated food, in addition to water, are amebiasis and cyclospora.

The single-celled parasite called *Entamoeba histolytica* causes the intestinal illness amebiasis (am-e-bye-a-sis). It is a common disease in developing countries with poor sanitary conditions. Most victims in the United States are recent immigrants, people who have contracted the illness traveling outside of the country, or those who live in poorly maintained housing facilities or work in unhygenic conditions.

The symptoms of amebiasis are usually mild, but the disease can progress to a severe form called amebic dysentery. With amebic dysentery, the victim may experience severe stomach pain, fever, and even damage to the lungs or brain. The parasite literally invades the body, where it grows and spreads. If left untreated, amebic dysentery can be fatal. People become infected with the parasite after swallowing contaminated food or water or by touching the cysts, which are the eggs of the parasite, and then accidentally bringing the eggs to the mouth. The cysts, invisible to the naked eye, could be present on surfaces contaminated with the parasite.

PARASITES

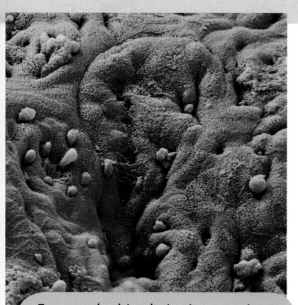

Entamoeba histolytica is a species of protozoa that causes amebiasis, with symptoms including cramping and diarrhea. This parasite most often inhabits tropical areas with poor sanitation.

Caused by the *Cyclospora cayetanensis* parasite, cyclospora was first identified in 1979. Since then, outbreaks of the disease have been reported in the United States and Canada. As with most parasitic protozoan diseases, it is spread by drinking contaminated water, by eating contaminated food, or by hand-to-mouth contact after touching a surface with the parasite on it.

It takes days, even weeks, for a person to feel the first symptoms of cyclospora, which causes intestinal problems. That is because the parasite multiplies in the body after passing through the liver. If left untreated, victims of the disease could suffer for a month or longer, during which time there may be periods of feeling better followed by relapses.

INSECTS: VECTORS FOR DISEASE

Insects and other animals that can spread disease are known as vectors. In virtually all cases, the insects themselves are not harmful unless present in large numbers. They are dangerous to animals and humans because of the parasites, bacteria, and other germs that they might carry and then transfer to bite victims.

Insect vectors for parasitic diseases fall into two groups. The first consists of mosquitoes and other flying, biting insects. These insects usually possess a mouthpart similar to a needle. They puncture the skin of victims and draw out blood. If the insect has parasites in its body, the parasite might spread into the victim's blood or lymphatic system during the bite. Diseases that might not otherwise travel easily from person to person can spread rapidly in the presence of biting insects. A mosquito, for example, might bite an infected person. That mosquito could then bite another person, and then another, spreading the parasitic disease.

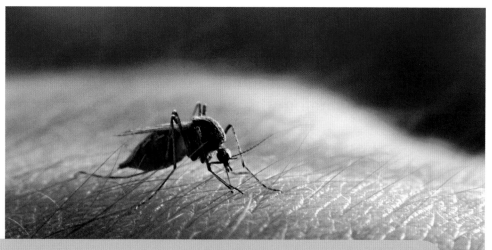

A mosquito sucks blood from a victim using its proboscis. Its food source makes it a vector of other parasitic organisms, rather than a true parasite itself.

THE PERILS OF MALARIA

Worldwide, malaria is one of the most serious and widespread parasitic diseases. It is spread by mosquitoes. It is said that more than 40 percent of the world's population is at risk. In the United States, most cases occur among immigrants and those who travel to areas where malaria is a concern.

Four types of parasites, four different species of plasmodium, an amoebalike microorganism, can lead to malaria. In each case, the parasites must grow in the mosquito for a week or more before an infection can be transmitted to a victim. After a person is infected by the parasites through a mosquito bite, the parasites travel to the liver, where they grow, multiply, and enter the individual's red blood cells, which later burst. Victims feel as though they have a terrible case of the flu. If not treated with prescription medication, one form of the disease can cause kidney failure and may even result in death. In some cases, the parasites can lay dormant, or remain inactive, in a person's liver for up to four years before the parasites revive, multiply, and cause illness.

BLOODSUCKERS: FLEAS, TICKS, AND OTHERS

While mosquitoes themselves are not parasites, fleas and ticks are. As adults, these wingless creatures must live on other creatures, such as birds and mammals, including humans, in order to survive. Unlike most mosquitoes, they can pose a health risk even if they are not infected with a parasitic bacteria or germ.

Both fleas and ticks feed on blood. They attach themselves to a host and then puncture the skin to draw out the nourishing blood. Because fleas and ticks rapidly multiply, they can weaken the host and cause anemia, an illness that may result from blood loss. The skin will often become inflamed and itchy, as bug mouthparts can become imbedded in the skin.

HOW TO SAFELY REMOVE A TICK

If you go camping or spend time outdoors, chances are good that you may become a host for a tick. As viruses and bacteria can be present in the tick's body, it is important to remove the tick carefully. This should be done with a pair of fine-tipped tweezers. Grasp the tick as close to the skin as you can and lift it out, being careful not to squeeze the tick's round body. It is a myth that lighting a match or using petroleum jelly will help. They can even do more harm because if the tick becomes irritated, it may tighten its grip and inject even more potentially dangerous fluid into the host.

PARASITES

This scanning electron micrograph (SEM) shows the fearsome-looking head of a cat flea. Its two mandibles (*bottom center*) are used to break a host's skin and suck its blood.

Fleas and ticks have been among the most common vectors for various viral and bacterial infections. Many of the insidious diseases known through human history to be spread by these creatures have, luckily, been largely eliminated in the modern era. These included pathogens like typhus, as well as more fearsome infections. The bacterium *Yersina pestis*, for example, was transmitted by fleas (as well as rodents with fleas on them) and was responsible for the devastating pandemic known as the Black Death, which may have killed as many as two hundred million people in fourteenth-century Europe.

CHAPTER 3

LICE OUTBREAKS AND WORM INFESTATIONS

Other common parasites are lice and certain types of worms. The latter are mostly known to affect human digestion, though not all—some afflict the blood, while others target other organ systems. Unlike the microscopic protozoa, lice and worms are usually both visible (if they are not hidden in the body) due to their larger size, especially in their larger, adult stages.

LICE

The parasitic insect known as a louse is so common that you probably know someone who has suffered from an infestation. Every year, anywhere from six to twelve million people contract head lice, a species of lice adapted to living on the human scalp and neck. Many victims are between three and ten years old. That is because children often play in close physical contact with each other, and the insects jump easily to a new host.

PARASITES

Lice spread only when there is direct contact with a person who has lice or with items that touched the infected person's hair. These items may include clothing, hats, combs, carpets, beds, pillows, couches, or bath towels. Often contact occurs during recess, sports, or at slumber parties and camping trips.

When lice move into someone's hair, they can go through their entire life cycle right on that person's head. Lice begin as nits, or eggs. The eggs look like yellow or white specks and can be confused with dandruff, or dried skin particles. The eggs attach to the hair shaft where they later hatch.

Upon hatching, the nit becomes a nymph. The nymph is a very small, flat-bodied, wingless insect. It requires blood to survive, so at this stage the lice attach themselves to the scalp and begin to feed. After about seven days, the nymphs mature into adult lice, which look like little whitish, six-legged sesame seeds. Lice are so dependent on humans for food and shelter that they will die within a day of falling off the host's head.

Symptoms of lice infestation include itching, a tickling feeling on the head, and visible signs of the parasites themselves. While relatively harm-

A female louse (the singular for lice) latches on to a human for its meal of blood. Lice live on their hosts' bodies or in their clothing and bedding. Three types thrive on the human head, body, and groin area.

less, lice are hardly welcome guests. They can lead to infections if scratching produces sores. The good news is that they are highly preventable. To avoid infestation, take care not to share combs, brushes, or hats with others. Take particular care not to come into contact with the head of a person you know is suffering from head lice. If you go on a sleepover, bring your own pillow, pillowcase, and sleeping bag or sheets.

If you do contract head lice, they are highly treatable with medicated shampoos, creams, and ointments. Usually a single application of medicine works. In some cases, lice can spread to the eyebrows and eyelashes, which may require special treatment by a doctor. Other types of lice can affect different parts of the body.

WORMS

Worms can be more dangerous to humans than lice because worms may live and multiply inside a person's body, unlike lice, which exclusively live on the skin's surface. It is important to remind yourself that a parasitic worm is very different from most worms that you find in the garden. Common garden worms are usually beneficial to humans because they help break down soil and keep it nutritious for crops and other plant life.

While soil worms feed on the organic matter in dirt, parasitic worms feed off whatever they infest, be it a fish or person. There are many different kinds of parasitic worms. Virtually all begin by feeding on food and other nutrients stored within the host's body. If this supply dwindles as the worms produce and multiply, the parasites may begin to feed on blood and other body fluids. When this happens, the host may suffer from anemia, infections, and other health problems.

There are four principal methods of transmission, or ways in which people can become infected with parasitic worms. Worms spread to humans through water, food, insect bites, and contaminated soil.

Most parasitic worms that live in water can also live in food. That is because particles of food or waste material may wind up in water, creating a breeding ground for parasitic worms. Municipal treatment facilities carefully filter water and use certain chemicals, like chlorine, to rid water of parasites and other contaminants. Contracting worms from water is not common in the United States and other developed countries. Use of improperly tested well water, however, can lead to parasitic diseases. Consuming water after a flood can as well. Swimming in contaminated water is another way in which parasites can spread to humans. Some worms spread when a person eats contaminated food or accidentally swallows parasitic worms after touching a contaminated surface. These are the most common ways to get infected, particularly in the United States.

Developed nations often keep many parasitic protozoa from spreading through the water supply through careful treatment. This water treatment plant cleans water before people use it for drinking, cooking, and bathing.

SCHISTOSOMIASIS

In certain parts of Africa, South America, the Caribbean, China, the Middle East, and Southeast Asia, some types of snails harbor parasitic worms called *Schistosoma*, or blood flukes, that cause a disease known as schistosomiasis. The parasites can penetrate the skin of a person who may be swimming or bathing in water where the snails live, and then enter the person's bloodstream.

Mild infections cause rash and flulike symptoms. In more severe cases, the parasites can travel to the brain and spinal cord. Such an infection can even cause paralysis. Other major organs may also be damaged. Thankfully there are prescription drugs that can kill the worms and clear up the infestation.

PARASITES

PINWORMS

One of the most prevalent infection-causing parasitic worms is the pinworm. This is a small white worm that resides in the human intestines. A sneaky worm, the pinworm leaves the intestines at night. Under the cover of darkness, females exit the body and lay eggs on the sleeping person's skin.

Young children are most often affected, as the worms often spread in child care centers, day camps, schools, and other places where close contact with victims might occur. Eggs laid on the skin can fall off and live for up to two weeks on clothes, bedding, and other objects. Usually a victim becomes infected after accidentally swallowing one or more of the microscopic eggs.

Because most pinworm infections are mild, many hosts for the worms show no symptoms, which can facilitate further spreading to other unsuspecting victims. Bad cases can lead to loss of appetite and difficulty sleeping, mostly due to the worm activity at night. Medicines taken over a two-week period can rid a person of the worms.

THE ASCARID WORM

The ascarid worm is similar to the pinworm and is by far the most common parasitic worm that bothers humans worldwide. In the United States, the presence of ascarids, small intestinal worms, usually occurs in rural areas of the Southeast. Among livestock, the animal most affected by ascarids, and parasitic worms in general, is the pig. That is because pigs eat close to the ground, may be fed contaminated food scraps, and spend a lot of time rolling around in dirt where the worms might reside.

TAPEWORMS AND ROUNDWORMS

If humans eat contaminated meat that has not been properly cooked, they can become infected with parasitic worms. Two types of worms spread by eating contaminated pork and beef are tapeworms and roundworms.

Tapeworms, which live in the small intestine of human hosts, can grow and reproduce for many years if left untreated. Some tapeworms may reach several feet in length. A single worm also can lay fifty eggs a day.

Trichinosis, caused by a roundworm, occurs when a person eats raw or undercooked pork infested by the parasitic worm. It causes everything from fever to heart problems. Trichinosis used to be common in the United States, but strict regulations on the way pigs are raised and butchered, and better recommendations for cooking pork, have nearly eliminated the problem.

This light micrograph shows the parasite known as *Trichinella spiralis*—also known as the pork roundworm. It is spread to victims when they eat meat containing cysts containing the parasite's larvae.

PARASITES

PROTECTING PETS FROM PARASITES

Dogs and cats commonly get tapeworms from fleas. The dog or cat, while grooming, may swallow an infected flea. Worms and eggs from the flea will then develop in the animal's intestinal tract. Aside from the presence of fleas, the clearest sign of infection is the presence of white or opaque rice-like specks near the pet's bottom. While usually not serious, worms should be treated because they can deplete the dog or cat of nutrients and can lead to stomach upset. Pet stores and even grocery stores usually carry dewormers (also known as wormers) for pets. These are drugs that can be administered as drops, injected, or even as a topical ointment. Veterinary help should be sought, however, for severe cases or if the animal is very young or old and needs help fighting the infestation.

INSECT BITES

Just as mosquitoes can transmit protozoa, these flying, biting vectors can also pass worms to people. Lymphatic filariasis (lim-fat-ick fil-uh-rye-uh-sis) affects more than 120 million people worldwide but does not occur in the United States. A threadlike worm that invades the lymphatic system causes the disease. In the United States, most parasitic worm infections happen after the ingestion of contaminated food and water and not through insect bites.

WORMS IN SOIL

One of the creepiest-looking intestinal parasites is the hookworm. The tip of a hookworm is a head with a giant open mouth full of sharp teethlike structures. They allow it to hook on to the walls of a human being's intestines, where it feeds. The eggs of the hookworm are passed through human feces or that of any animal infected with them. People can get the worm by walking barefoot in contaminated soil, or, in the case of certain types, by accidentally swallowing the larval form of the worm. Those infected with the worm for the first time are most likely to have gastrointestinal problems, but many who carry hookworms exhibit no symptoms.

The United States and other Western nations have largely eliminated hookworm infestation. Still, it continues to affect tens of millions of victims worldwide every year. Doctors can prescribe medication to kill these worms, but supplies are limited in poorer nations, especially those where the need is greatest because poor sanitation systems expose many millions to human waste in the open air.

Ancylostoma duodenale, also known as the Old World hookworm, lives in the intestines of animals like cats, dogs, and human beings. Severe cases can cause extreme protein or iron deficiencies.

CHAPTER 4

THE PARASITE CYCLE

Prescription medications are among the best treatments for parasitic infections. However, for many people, these may have unpleasant side effects. For many others, these medicines can be expensive or hard to come by. Hence, the best offense is a good defense: preventing parasites from taking root in one's body in the first place. The first step is understanding the life cycles of typical parasites.

A TAPEWORM'S LIFE

Tapeworms are a common parasite that may infest humans. They can spread in many different ways. Let's examine the life of a tapeworm now living in a big fish and how it might spread and impact humans.

A fisherman on a camping trip catches a fish in a lake. He cooks it briefly over a camp stove and eats the fish for dinner. The tapeworm, having survived the brief cooking, grows and reproduces inside the unknowing fisherman. Human waste, containing tapeworm eggs, winds up in the soil and washes back into the lake. The eggs hatch and mature into adult tapeworms. A copepod, a type of crustacean, such as a small shrimp, swims by and eats the tapeworm. A small fish eats the shrimp. Later, an even bigger fish eats the small fish. At this point, the tapeworm has matured and multiplied, with the big fish now serving as host. A large animal, such as a human or a bear, catches and eats the fish and the cycle begins all over again. Another camper could drink water from the lake and become infected and start another life cycle for the tapeworm.

A man holds up a bottle filled with water from Ethiopia's Omo River, which is consumed by local people. Water quality is one of the greatest challenges to limiting parasitic infections throughout the world.

PREVENTION AND CONTROL

As the tapeworm life cycle demonstrates, parasites can pass to humans through water, food, and soil. An infected mosquito can also pass on a parasite through its bite. While there are many different kinds of parasites that multiply quickly, it is possible to stop the cycle from reaching humans.

PARASITES

Tap water in the United States must meet certain standards, so infection from municipal water is rare. If you are drinking untreated water, during a hike or camping trip, for example, or if you are traveling to countries without proper water treatment facilities, water still can be made safe to drink.

Boiling water for a minute or more usually kills any parasites that might be present. Iodine tablets, available at most pharmacies and sporting goods' stores, also can kill parasites when the tablets are dissolved in water. Filters containing iodine can be used to protect against protozoa and worms.

When traveling outside of the United States to countries with known water problems, it is best to drink canned or bottled beverages. Avoid ice, as many parasites can survive below the freezing point of water. Boiled water drinks, like tea, are safer.

Even if you have not traveled much outside the country, you, or someone you know, probably have experienced a bout of food poisoning. A parasite, bacteria, or toxin in the food could have caused the problem. Since heat kills most of these microscopic, living organisms, chances are that the food was undercooked, raw, or allowed to stand for some time without being reheated before it was eaten. Fish, shellfish, and meat are especially problematic because they can contain parasites and their eggs.

Be sure to thoroughly cook foods, as instructed on the packaging or in a cookbook. Fish, for example, requires less cooking time than pork, which must be heated to a certain internal temperature. When storing foods for transport, keep hot foods hot and cold foods cold using a thermos or some other special, protective container.

A cruise ship docks in Fort Lauderdale, Florida. *Cyclospora cayetanensis*, a protozoan, has been known to cause the stomach ailment cyclosporiasis on cruises. Illness outbreaks on cruises have been mostly viral, however.

When eating in countries with poor sanitation, avoid salads, other raw vegetable and fruit dishes, and unpasteurized milks and cheeses. Salads, for example, may have been washed with contaminated water. Also take care when purchasing food from street vendors. Make sure the food is fresh and heated before eating.

PARASITES

SUSHI AND RAW FOODS: SAFETY CONCERNS

Given all of the health risks associated with raw fish and meats, it may seem surprising to some that dishes like sushi, often made with raw fish and shellfish, and steak tartare, an uncooked meat dish, are so popular worldwide. Quality restaurants and markets hire trained professionals who can distinguish fresh meats and fish that are safe to eat raw from those that might be contaminated. When in doubt, select foods that have been cooked, as heating kills most parasites and germs.

One fishborne parasite that is less common in the United States but more common overseas is *Anisakis simplex*, a roundworm whose larvae can infect raw or undercooked seafood. It causes anisakiasis, a condition in which the worm tries to penetrate the sufferer's intestinal wall and gets stuck and dies. The immune system responds, with the body's cells forming a ball around the dead worm that blocks digestive function, leading to severe abdominal pain, vomiting, and malnutrition.

PREVENTING INFECTION FROM PARASITIC INSECTS AND VECTORS

The best way to prevent being bitten by a mosquito, flea, tick, or other animal associated with parasites is to avoid the biting bugs. Most disease-spreading mosquitoes are active at dawn or dusk, when temperatures are not too warm or cold. You may have even noticed that more mosquitoes fly around outside your home during these times. It is then that they are likely to feed on unsuspecting hosts, like humans.

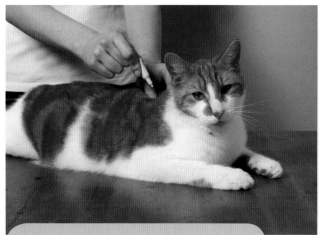

Flea and tick infestation in animals can be irritating to the animal and threaten owners, too. Most outbreaks are easily prevented or treated.

Fleas and ticks are a bit harder to track down. They can exist in certain rural areas, in tall brush or grass, or even in the fur of a family pet. Since it is impossible to completely avoid mosquitoes and other insects, sometimes other precautionary measures are necessary. Be sure to regularly wash the bedding of dogs and cats. Keep the animals well brushed and groomed. Bathe them when necessary. Cats do not always require baths, so check with your veterinarian first to ask about your specific pet.

When in outdoor areas where mosquitoes and parasitic insects are prevalent, wear protective clothing. Bugs cannot bite through most clothing, so anything that is covered will receive some protection. In rural places where there are a lot of fleas and ticks, pant legs can be tucked into socks, which will prevent fleas and ticks from touching your skin.

A number of insect repellents are available, even in grocery stores. Use them with the guidance of adults and only when protection from clothing and other methods are not enough. Also check the ingredients to see that they contain no harmful chemicals. Repellents containing permethrin, a natural substance made from chrysanthemum flowers, can last for several days when sprayed on shoes and clothing.

TWENTY-FIRST CENTURY PARASITES

Modern research, medicines, and other tools in the war against parasitic diseases help to keep parasites under control. Current problems, such as pollution, overpopulation, bioterrorism, and climate change, however, often work in favor of parasites. The quality of water, food, and soil all suffer when under stresses that upset the natural balance. A fish weakened from bacteria present in a polluted lake, for example, would be more vulnerable to infestation by parasites. It is therefore important to address problems that affect the ecosystem.

While they are rightfully considered a serious threat to human health throughout the world, scientists believe parasites and their life cycles can provide lessons that will improve medical knowledge. Researchers are investigating how tapeworms and other parasites survive in adverse environments—including the inhospitable surroundings of the human digestive sys-

tem—and hope to use this information to improve pharmaceu-
ticals, treat different kinds of illnesses, and also to cure parasitic
infections themselves. One aim is to design drugs that can with-
stand extreme conditions using the defense mechanisms and
physical makeup of parasites as an example. If these projects
yield results, parasites may inadvertently contribute to helping
as well as harming humanity.

A municipal truck sprays a mosquito pesticide called Scourge on a
country road in Covington, Louisiana, mainly in an effort to prevent
and minimize the spread of the West Nile virus.

GLOSSARY

AMEBIASIS A food and waterborne disease caused by parasitic protozoa.

APICOMPLEXAN A type of parasitic protozoan; many of which cause disease.

ARACHNID An animal possessing eight legs and a body divided into three parts.

CILIATE A type of protozoan that propels itself with small hairs.

CRYPTOSPORIDIOSIS A waterborne disease caused by parasitic protozoa.

CYCLOSPORA A food and waterborne disease caused by parasitic protozoa.

FLAGELLATES Protozoa with tail-like extensions to assist in movement.

FLEA A wingless insect that feeds on blood from a host.

GIARDIASIS A waterborne disease caused by parasitic protozoa.

HOST The organism that a parasite lives in or on.

MALARIA A serious and widespread disease spread by mosquitoes carrying parasitic protozoa.

MUTUALISM A relationship in which two organisms interact and both benefit from the relationship.

PARASITE An organism that lives in or on another living creature and benefits from it without providing anything in return.

PROTOZOA Single-celled microscopic creatures that usually can move by themselves.

SARCODINES Protozoa with a toelike appendage for loco-motion; many have protective shells.

SCHISTOSOMIASIS A disease caused by a parasitic worm.

TAPEWORM A common form of parasitic worm that can grow to be several feet in length.

TICK An arachnid that feeds on blood from a host.

VECTOR An organism, such as an insect, that can spread disease.

WORMS Animals with soft, thin bodies and without back-bones or ribs.

FOR MORE INFORMATION

American Museum of Natural History
Division of Invertebrate Zoology
Central Park at 79th St.
New York, NY 10024
(212) 769-5100
Website: http://www.amnh.org/our-research/invertebrate-zoology
The Division of Invertebrate Zoology at the American Museum
of Natural History studies and archives the living nonverte-
brate animals, which make up 95 percent of all animal species.
It houses more than twenty-four million specimens, which
comprises about five hundred thousand species.

American Society of Parasitologists
c/o John Hopkins Bloomberg School of Public Health
615 North Wolfe Street
Baltimore, MD
Website: http://amsocparasit.org
The American Society of Parasitologists (ASP) is a diverse group
of more than eight hundred scientists from industry, government, and academia who are interested in the study and teach-
ing of parasitology.

Association of Medical Microbiology and Infectious Disease
Canada (AMMI)
192 Bank Street
Ottawa K2P 1W8
Canada
(613) 260-3233
info@ammi.ca

Website: http://www.ammi.ca

The Association of Medical Microbiology and Infectious Disease Canada (AMMI) promotes the prevention, diagnosis, and treatment of human infectious diseases through its involvement in education, research, clinical practice, and patient advocacy.

National Institutes of Health (NIH)
9000 Rockville Pike
Bethesda, MD 20892
(301) 496-4000
NIHinfo@od.nih.gov
Website: http://www.nih.gov

The National Institutes of Health (NIH) is a research facility in the Washington, DC, area that is the primary agency of the United States government in charge of biomedical and health-related research.

Office of Health Communication
National Center for Infectious Diseases
The Centers for Disease Control and Prevention
Mailstop C-14
1600 Clifton Road
Atlanta, GA 30333
Website: http://www.cdc.gov

The Centers for Disease Control and Prevention (CDC) is the primary United States government agency in charge of tracking, treating, and preventing public health threats, including infectious diseases.

World Health Organization (WHO)
Avenue Appia 20
1211 Geneva 27
Switzerland
Website: http://www.who.int/en
The World Health Organization (WHO) is the specialized agency of the United Nations that is primarily concerned with international public health.

WEBSITES

Because of the changing number of Internet links, Rosen Publishing has developed an online list of websites related to the subject of this book. This site is updated regularly. Please use this link to access this list:

http://www.rosenlinks.com/GDCO/para

FOR FURTHER READING

Despommier, Dickson D. *People, Parasites, and Plowshares: Learning from Our Body's Most Terrifying Invaders*. New York, NY: Columbia University Press, 2016.

Drisdelle, Rosemary. *Parasites: Tales of Humanity's Most Unwelcome Guests*. Berkeley, CA: University of California Press, 2010.

Dunn, Rob. *The Wild Life of Our Bodies: Predators, Parasites, and Partners That Shape Who We Are Today*. New York, NY: Harper-Collins, 2014.

Gardenour, Brenda, and Misha Tadd (Eds.). *Parasites, Worms, and the Human Body in Religion and Culture*. New York, NY: Peter Lang Publishing, 2012.

Gittleman, Ann Louise. *Guess What Came to Dinner? Parasites and Your Health*. New York, NY: Avery Books, 2001.

Grove, David. *Tapeworms, Lice, and Prions: A Compendium of Unpleasant Infections*. New York, NY: Oxford University Press, 2014.

Lew, Kristi. *Food Poisoning: E. Coli and the Food Supply* (Headlines!). New York, NY: Rosen Publishing, 2011.

Patten, Barbara J. *Food Safety: Food for Good Health*. Vero Beach, FL: Rourke Publishing, LLC, 1995.

Snodgrass, Mary Ellen. *Environmental Awareness: Water Pollution*. Marco, FL: Bancroft-Sage Publishing Incorporated, 1991.

Tilden, Thomasine E. Lewis. *Belly-Busting Worm Invasions! Parasites That Love Your Insides!* (24/7: Science Behind the Scenes: Medical Files). New York, NY: Children's Press, 2010.

Zimmer, Carl. *Parasite Rex: Inside the Bizarre World of Nature's Most Dangerous Creatures*. New York, NY: Atria Books, 2001.

BIBLIOGRAPHY

Drexler, Madeline. *Secret Agents: The Menace of Emerging Infections.* Washington, DC: Joseph Henry Press, 2002.

Dye, Lee. "Sticking Around: Tapeworm Could Hold Key to Getting Meds to Stay in Digestive System." ABCNews.com, March 12, 2003.

Moore, Janice. *Parasites and the Behavior of Animals* (Oxford Series in Ecology and Evolution). New York, NY: Oxford University Press, 2002.

Morand, Serge, and Boris R. Krasnov. *The Biogeography of Host-Parasite Interactions.* New York, NY: Oxford University Press, 2010.

Simon, Hilda. *Partners, Guests, and Parasites: Coexistence in Nature.* New York, NY: Viking Penguin, 1970.

Sharma, Rajenda. *The Family Encyclopedia of Health.* Boston, MA: Element Books Limited, 1998.

World Health Organization. "World Malaria Report 2015." Retrieved January 2, 2016 (http://www.who.int/malaria/publications/world-malaria-report-2015/wmr2015-without-profiles.pdf?ua=1).

INDEX

A
anemia, 21, 26
apicomplexans, 8, 9
arachnids, 7, 11–12

B
bacteria, 4, 19, 21, 22, 34, 38

C
ciliates, 8, 9
cryptosporidiosis, 15, 16
cyclospora, 17, 18

F
flagellates, 8, 9
flatworms, 9–10
fleas, 11, 12, 20–22, 30, 36, 37
flukes, 10, 27

G
giardiasis, 15–16

L
lice, 5, 11, 23–25

M
malaria, 4–5, 9, 20
medications, 32, 38
    for hookworm, 31
    for lice, 25
    for malaria, 20
    for pinworms, 28
micropredators, 11
mites, 5, 11

mosquitoes, 4, 11, 19, 20, 21, 30, 33, 36–37
mutualism, 13

P
preventing parasitic infections, 25, 32, 33–35, 36–38
protozoa, 5, 7, 8–9, 14, 23, 30, 34
    diseases of, 15, 18
    foodborne, 17–18
    parasites, 11–12

R
ribbon worms, 9, 10
roundworms, 10, 29, 36

S
sarcodines, 8, 9
symbiosis, 7, 13

T
tapeworms, 10, 29, 30, 32–33, 38–39
ticks, 11, 20–22, 36, 37

V
vectors, for disease, 18–19, 22, 30, 36–38

W
worms, 25–26, 30, 34
    ascarid, 28–29
    intestinal, 5, 28
    parasitic, 26, 27, 28, 29, 30
    segmented, 9, 10, 11
    in soil, 9, 31

ABOUT THE AUTHORS

Margaux Baum is a young adult nonfiction author from Queens, New York. She has written numerous books for Rosen Publishing covering disease prevention, drug addiction, and science.

Jennifer Viegas is a reporter for Discovery News, the news service for the Discovery Channel. She also is a features columnist for Knight Ridder newspapers.

PHOTO CREDITS